# All You Have In Common

Books by Dara Wier

*Blood, Hook & Eye* (1977)
*The 8-Step Grapevine* (1980)
*All You Have In Common* (1984)

# All You Have In Common

*12/12/84*
*Tuscaloosa*

*For Peter,*

*With good wishes,*

## poems by

*T. Dara Wier*

## Dara Wier

Carnegie-Mellon University Press
Pittsburgh 1984
Feffer and Simons, Inc., London

## ACKNOWLEDGEMENTS

Grateful acknowledgement is made to the following publications in which these poems first appeared. "Late Afternoon on a Good Lake," *American Poetry Review;* "The Innate Deception of Unspoiled Beauty," *The Black Warrior Review;* "Faith," "Here," "Sleeping in Cars," *Cimarron Review;* "All You Have In Common," *Columbia: a magazine of the Arts;* "The Moon and Not Japan," *Cyphers;* "You Whose Body Has Never Touched Another Body," "Colorless, Green Ideas," *Forum;* "Fear," "Holidays," *The Missouri Review;* "Where There Was Stillness," *North American Review;* "The Consequence of Weather," Palaemon Press broadside series, number 21; "The Batture," "Memory," "That Which Was Originally Sacred," *The Poetry Miscellany.*

I would like to thank the National Endowment for the Arts for a fellowship in poetry which gave me time to begin this book.

The book's epigraph is from Shakespeare's Sonnet 84. The epigraph which begins "Where There Was Stillness," is from Rainer Marie Rilke's *The Rodin-Book.*

*The publication of this book is supported by grants from the National Endowment for the Arts in Washington D. C., a Federal agency, and the Pennsylvania Council on the Arts. Books in the Carnegie-Mellon University Press Poetry Series are distributed by the University of Pittsburgh Press, 127 N. Bellefield Avenue, Pittsburgh, Pennsylvania 15260.*

**Library of Congress Catalog Card Number 84-70179**
**ISBN 0-88748-004-7**
**ISBN 0-88748-005-5 Pbk.**

# CONTENTS

*for Michael*

*Who is it that says most? Which can say more*
*Than this rich praise, that you alone are you?*

## *HERE*

*Then let's compare.*
*There are so many ways*

*to take it, here,*
*take it with you when you go.*

Here *I take my seat*
*in the classroom row.*

*Here, not that, here, here.*
*Here are the hours.*

*Here, take what you like.*
*Here, forgive the loans.*

*Here, count what you're given.*
*When you listen to the song*

*I'd like to give you everything*
*you'd ever want,*

*diamond rings for every toe,*
*dangling earrings for your fingers,*

*big sparkling rocks*
*for your nose you know*

*the singer doesn't mean it.*
*Put your hands between my breasts, here.*

## FEAR

In fall when we went the roads
for the pure reason of pretending
we were still and the world fell
away all around us, the dry fall
kept my tongue circling my lips.
Think how many paths
circles cross. What range
the tongue bringing moisture
to chapped skin laps.
I watched my grandfather rub
petroleum jelly on his hearing aid
ear. Each of his possessions,
package of black tobacco,
jar of mentholatum,
and, collapsed around a gold coin
he never let me touch,
a leather pouch soft
as damp moss, greygreen,
a lesson. He leaned
and touched his hearing aid
battery to my mouth
to burn my lips, a silver spot
of circular burn that comes back,
*do you regret knowing*
*he took your hands around his testicles*
*when it is easy to believe*
*those nights taught you*
*how one thing becomes another.*
His back had been a thing burnt
black when he was brought home
from the clinic to recover
from anthrax. I would not touch
a thing he touched. I watched
the black crescents his fingernails
drew as he drew melon seeds
from cotton sacks or wrapped raffia
around the wounds his knife drew

for citrus grafts.
When he squeezed ichthyol salve
on my instep to draw the thick thorn
back, it healed.
The cusp of the deer's hoof
is static in our headlights.
There, a blow we've taken,
movement in shadow near the road;
we've shied, recovered,
and watch for other dangers.
There is the rabbit
whose carelessness could kill us
but she freezes in our headlights
for the next car coming or the random
truck whose driver has no thought
for her or us. Think how many
times it's crossed your mind,
will they kill us, will the deer
rushing across the road for water
batter his neck on the windshield,
will your swerve to miss another skunk
land us in a ditch. What's out there
eager to satisfy need or desire
does not care, knows nothing
about the paths we cross.
My tongue without thinking
drives back another wad of tobacco
to soothe a black jacket's sting.
Think of the traffic a tongue congests,
how the heart crosses and compares
what might not have been
drawn together. Under a perfectly beautiful
moon and on its opening evening
the new highway kills eleven dogs
in its suprising traffic.

# THE DARK SIDE OF THE MOON

We've been asked to sign up
to meet on the dark side

of the full moon. We knew
this would happen when

you mention tequila is spilling
and it never misses

when I start to say
I'm not afraid

a certified lunatic
writes *Do not say*

*you have no fear.*
The celestial bodies

are turning to welcome
us with banners of red

streamers they may
change my mind

I'm about to say
go alone we could live

in two different worlds
*some other time* but we do.

It's the lunatic moon
of the kamikaze or the perfect

binge of what is this,
this and the suprise of the other side.

# THE INTERCESSION OF LIGHT

It is light moving
toward you or shadow moving
over you.

The field might be a sheet
shaken at the hands
of a luminous blonde.

It just might belly up.

Never in your life have you
been touched as you have just been
touched by light

as it moves the mown field
or the gray slate of the tilted
cliff.

If the light raced, reared
on desire, the need to go anywhere
fast, it would rid itself

of the random cause of its loveliness.
If it returned, you would rid yourself
of whatever it is that keeps you

attentive to the twists and turn,
the sudden cause of your desire
to give up,

to lose yourself,
lie down in the field
and be shaken.

## THE BATTURE

The batture's water and sand disappear
when water swells the river,
heat's portion of a northern winter.
Under willows cropped up
since our last cow is dead
and carried to the batture
to be taken by the water
clean into another season,
we sit on green granite
piled deep enough to keep
the batture dry one more week.

We don't say so but we wait
for the swollen body
to appear before us, we want
the torn leg to distract us,
the loose arm to show us where.
We've always known which way
the water runs, the differences
among earth, air, water
and whatever the horizon offers
that is not actually there.
We want to be the ones
to identify the missing person.
We count the reward we'd earn.

There is a family
in southern Minnesota
keeping a closet of dry-cleaned
suits, a mahogany high-boy
of ironed shirts, folded
undershorts and sweaters.
In the ashtray that says *Welcome to Nevada*
are the coins he left
without thinking,
the only clue which tells his family

what they didn't want to know,
he might have known
what he was doing.

We want to be the ones whose call
is first in a series of related events
which will end we hope in the family's
satisfaction with the coroner's
identification, and though it is old-fashioned
and no longer done in this country,
we'd like to think the pennies
from his pocket will be mailed
to the morgue, polished to
their copper finish, pressed
to float forever on his eyelids and make us
take a second look as the light
hits them and they beautifully glitter.

We think how glad we were
when we first saw him he floated
face down in the water
which a few months earlier had been snow
his children sledded and slipped on.
Light beats gravity, lifts
these young trees from the water.
This is where we watch time,
mark the spot across the water
which is the red flag
we hope calls us
*come across and save us.*
This is twenty-eight states.

## PLAY

The laws of gravity,
light and property
are not laws to us.
Our tongues swarm
in our wet mouths.
When the finger is
slipped in the skull
to the knuckle'
we think this is it
we stack the letters
of the alphabet
and don't notice
because this is what
we've been waiting for
when they tumble
to assemble *on, saw,*
*sea, ease,* the pieces
of our puzzles
take the shape
of everything around;
because it doesn't burn
in this world
we'll never know
or care beyond
it isn't electric
because we don't feel it
the beauty of building
something that tumbles
harmlessly down.
We are moving
a purple rubber ball
we don't have to remember
because its red, black
and blue stars swarm
with love of this
planet, because it
never ends, because
it is so round.

## ALL YOU HAVE IN COMMON

Your friend keeps writing, showing
it to a nun who is murmuring
*put your little foot right here.*
She is a movie star picking out
from your trunk full of props
a grosgrain ribbon.

The year the prickly pear passed
its first river barrier, the book began.
The house, old, the man living there
leaving to join an army.

A sound is coming with the light.
It is heat that beats the crickets'
wings to pieces.
Your father, leaning against a rake,
mistakes them for leaves.

The moving men mistake your house,
the one on the hill, for another house.
There goes your trunk.
*Because it surprises you, you know
it is your imagination.*

The woman in the swimsuit, swimming
like a bird in a dustbowl, bathing,
waves you away. Your damp hands
will only tattoo her with earth.
She couldn't stand it. *So go on.*

Get back to the movies. You want to know
who it is with the president's daughter.
It is the nun. She is only trying
to clean up her habit.
She wishes you would ignore her.

Wishes you would instead, concentrate
on the road map, your lap.
Wishes you would notice sooner
the soft ruts in the road.
Remember there is a lady reclined in each river.

You think you've finally gotten the moving men
to the right house. But in this place, *even you*
*keep forgetting what's what.*
You are showing a man, his arms a cradle of cactus,
weak spots in the house's construction.

A woman appears from the fabric shop.
She keeps showing you ribbons, the lovely wings
of crickets, their golden sequins and glitter.
What curtains! But you are moving out.

Once your father sees the shining crickets,
he goes fishing.
You can't seem to knot the hook just right.
Your father says put the hook right here.
Put so the cricket will still waddle.

Put so it appears to be stroking, gently
closing and opening like perfect venetian blinds.
The bars upon which this quiet song sits.
That song. The one you were singing
to your friend, dancing, dangling her legs
in the dust, in the water.

Stop worrying you'll get your costume wet.
*Stop telling his lies.*
And the three women. What they all have
in common: their houses emptied, their bare floors
sparkle, floors of balsa, their breathing
lighter than balsa, than air.

They walk from their houses toward a basket,
held by your father, alive with the moving
mouths of small insects.
One woman is a lip reader.
The other speaks with her hands.
One tries climbing without dropping her hat in the river.
They dress in swimsuits and simmering, swim in their sleep.

*You can keep this up as long as you want.*
As long as you, as the man sleeping with you,
keep singing that song.
*Put your little foot right here.*

The books in your arms, the ones you pulled
from the trunk, are the sinkers. Be careful
to recognize the bait. *That is one thing
you don't want to do to yourself.*

But the narrator keeps calling your name.
You are the one who drives the moving van.
The nun keeps fixing her face in your rearview mirror.
She has starched her wimple.
It is clean like communion, like your friends' houses,
emptied.

It is 3:30. There are the crickets.
The afternoon light puts your father's chin on his chest.
You pat his back to make him rest
but your patting puts his chin too close
to his heart. His shadow, swimming there,
nearly drowns him.

The feathers you give him, from the cool
soft rut of a dustbowl's road, absorb the water.
And he keeps sinking. The water is warmer.
The wind turns the river up grinning.

But we are nearly to South Dakota.
The badlands' big ruts will hold this and more.
Why would we want to lie down
when the canyons could take us dancing?

The radio told us one thing, a tune hummed
that should have been whistled,
we think we know what it was.

## TROUBLE

Who keeps making up
questions too hard

to answer? The doctor
who puts his finger on it

says bad eyesight might be
the beginning.

Two to six inches of ice
will take down pines

and bust the magnolia's
beautiful snarled branches.

We're afraid we're still hard
at work in our busted houses,

we haven't learned our lessons,
we still don't like each other

enough. Reason's
stake is wrong

if it thinks
it'll bury itself

in our blood-sucking
hearts, it can forget

what it's taken
for evidence. Let's take

the cure, cooling
the vapors that rise

from hot waters,
let's make provisions,

let's have the doctor
set the table with knives.

Let's every day eat the forbidden
apples even out of season,

because we can't be certain,
be certain we'll decide

to be deadly, to be thorns,
we'll take sides.

# THAT WHICH WAS ORIGINALLY SACRED

You find it hard to believe Sister Sebastian
remembers your birthdate, harder to believe
the silver cross she sends you parcel post.
This gift has crossed eleven borders.
There is the cancellation.
Tied to the silver cross
which will tie the cross
to hang in the hollow
formed by your scapula and clavicle,
that delicate indentation
which can take your breath away,
comes the greeting:
This is dust. Earth from
the sacred ground of the catacomb
beneath Basilica St. Sebastiano.
A third class relic.
Touched. There is reason to believe
this dust is blessed.

The silver cross rests on your table.
When you watch it through a clear glass of water
you recall Sister Sebastian the first time
you felt a larger fear
when you stood with her on the playground
and the wind lifted her veil
over her face which was next to yours
and you looked at one another
in her brief black tent
while around you your friends'
shoes shocked the clay,
their hands hard to bounce a ball.
Your confused head and hers
head-on, she turned her face
and did nothing but confuse you further
in the twisted black cloth

which touched her cheek.
This time the wind didn't help,
she had to fix the veil herself
and scowled at you for standing
where you stood so close to her
to be the one to see
light rush from her face
as darkness rushes away
when struck by light
while the other children stopped
their game and knew now what
to make of her red and braided hair.

# DREAMLAND

It's not really enough
to want and to believe
because you've said it:
these aren't the sturdy ribs of pigs
I'm eating, these are the ribs of flamingos.
The Gulf is rarely crystal blue,
it is the Gulf of Mexico,
full of oil and bananas, important
to shipping, balmy and warm.
Lay back your hungry ears,
be reckless as a sponge is.
There's a bucket and it's glass
on the bottom so you see
right where you're falling
the sauce is so sweet, maybe
too sweet you think
it's the kind of sauce
that loves to drench the meat.
Your desire is indefatigable,
it oils the pattern
of your white shirt's fabric.
It's impossible to stop yourself.
You want to rub the sauce
on your chest. You want to eat
your shirt in public.
You want to be able and careful,
you want to keep your balance
but there's someone sculling
the boat that's carrying you
and your bucket and waiting
for you is the entire
crew of Greek sailors
who are tired themselves
after so long without surprises,
nothing but the buckets and buckets

of the puzzles of science, more
valuable as they pass from hand
to hand, as their futures sharpen
like stakes driven up beyond the needs
and pleasures of the real living bodies
stacking up on the deck. The poor sailors
will have to stomp the living sauce
under their bare and beautiful feet.
Vulcan bathed with a sponge. Venus
must have touched that sponge
one sailor thinks
as he kicks up his feet
another sailor picks up the drift
and sails into the clear blue
Gulf air. The whole deck shines,
the ribs of the sailors
are the polished ribs
of flamingos in flight,
inexhaustible and light, durable,
light and inexhaustible.

## BUZZARDS' ROOST

I'm in the middle
of no where near

the mirage of a border
but it's a fine morning.

The sun is huge
like the bull's eye

I imagine it looks
like no other

bull's eye I've seen.
Even the trees speak

in green tongues,
I hope they're sympathetic.

I like an old woman
fanning herself with Jesus

on Easter morning.
When I hear cards shuffle

I look over my shoulder
and blow some kisses

to the slow dealer
who doesn't cut.

I see the fan blades
flapping away the morning

I rose up to move
but raised my chair legs

over my head
and into the blades

which broke ring by ring
into scattered pieces.

I took out two eyes,
I pierced an innocent heart

with the mess I made.
I couldn't do anything

but be glad
I didn't start a fire.

I don't know how I'd behave
in a fire. I'm still

walking toward the river
when over my head

trees full of buzzards
shake off their sleep.

They scare me to death
in this exploded view

they dust off
their unmendable feathers.

# BREATH AND DEPTH OF FIELD

Breath, as it leaves the seam of lips,
leaves something, prepares
shafts of sun to slip in curtain folds.

In drouth snakes stole toward human damp,
found their way to teapots and cool twists
in basement windows where some moisture lingered.

Citizens started counting, the obsessed
searched their consciences, ordinary turns
of daily living were concerns outweighing death.

Where light and dark advance, depart,
what is touched, green as gardenia buds,
has also been tapped, new seeds firmly tamped.

Before the light of the kitchen lamp
you look like a monk, priest, penitent,
the shaft of dark which parts the one disguise
light has ever had to offer.

# A BORDER STATE SEES ITS COLDEST SEASON

You saw me safe to stand on ice.
We touched the split shore, pried

smooth chunks to pitch across the lake.
It is night. We live in different

climates. Your whip-poor-will cries
more than mine will sing in a week.

This is the first time I've stood
on ice. Because of this I keep quiet.

We hear in this land between, not
north, not south, see us

we stand in the middle, the loud
shot, the ice breaks, but it takes

its own good time dividing.
In any other life I'd think

I was dying, while this certain touch
of toe to boot to solid ice

teaches me to trust the steady hand,
to walk where I never knew to think.

# A SECRET MATTER OF GRAVE IMPORTANCE

Except when once we drew identical lots
nothing's ever come between us.
We keep our drifts of space
spare and daily shake our down.

You've glanced beyond your dirty cuffs
and caught me hand-washing my clean shirts.
Struck with sharp wind, both
bloods are rare and rarely do

we taste the walnut's knot of oil.
We wake between our fitted sheets
and shake our fists or pretend real fright
but not in this do we dare touch.

My rib cage can stand in yours, yours
become the swinging doors through which
magician's swords will slice and miss
that knotted muscle. It is a trick.

We'll make an endless show of the outright
clanking, irregular beating of our acrobatic hearts.
We've designed the double bars of depth;
our hearts skip — the tumbleset we think

is absence, the somersault we call forbearance
— the hearts are there, doing turns that teach
us to count and keep each finger
close to its own sly pulse.

## MEMORY

You have broken memory's chain
link line, say you remember
nothing of your childhood, you
don't care to try.
The choice you'd made
was to leave well enough alone.
The sequence of events was best let
to seek its own level,
in this case, sunk in a water
you failed to reason
was bound to dissolve.
Even water's attempt to be
what it is, water, burns
enough to change it.
You have asked why some of us
look over our shoulders
as if we might recognize
a difference. You've doubted
when we say eyes keep watch
from the backs of our heads.
You will always be lying
as long as you forget
and the rest of us remember

you spinning on the speckled linoleum floor
you shine until your thighs turn raw,

you sliding across the concrete playground
leaving the skin of your forearms and shins,

you trying to make sense of the bleeding
you take to be a sign of grief,

you stealing the ripe ox-heart tomato,
its magic act, a seed-sorter's accident,

you reaching for the saltine in the hand
you know is an extended greeting,

you licking your lips to stop the burn
bird's-eye peppers leave you, dupe of an easy trick,

you swimming under clean covers in the dark
you hunt for prizes in the game fishing for oysters,

you running afraid over the wooden bridge wishing
for wings to save you from the ugly animal under it,

you looking in the barrel in whose inner circle
you see your hurt dog bleeding on hay you gathered,

you, shaking your temperature down to normal

hoping to loosen the fever
of having to stay in the home
you are in a constant state
of leaving.
When you wish too hard
and hit your arm
the thermometer cracks, what was
a straight line comes apart
and you are faced with a thousand
silver balls which multiply
when you touch them, each one
smaller, more shimmering, each one
moving with a life of its own
over your flannel pajamas
and in the creases of your sickbed sheets.
You lie when you are asked
did you do that, explain
it cracked between your teeth.
Knowing mercury can poison, you
spit it from your mouth
and spend the last few minutes
chasing what can't by fever-weakened
hands be caught.

## HOLIDAYS

How many times our hands will enter
water to brighten our faces,
wash our glasses, clean our plates,
to rush through the turkey's carcass,
clean it of fat and blood,
whatever offends. We have gathered
to tell about the worlds we've left
to gather and tell of ourselves.

Your grandmother has recently lost
her husband. This is the first
time you remember her quiet,
letting herself be helped.
This is her daughter's house.
The last time she visited ten years
ago for your wedding. It is odd to see
your grandmother's hands out of water.

Your sister spells out the duties
of her latest part-time job, a gopher
for circuit court judges.
It is better than hamburgers,
better than the graveyard shift.
It's easy to fill an urn
with water for coffee, take down
brief messages from callers.

Your brother tells of gallons
of water he drank in Arizona,
fossil water, once secret
and hidden in the earth for centuries,
tapped for a growing population
in need of a clean source
of water for table flowers and
bright green squares of soft lawn.

Your other brother puts on the table
a rock the size of your dead grandfather's

fist, covered with lumps, having
the look of a brain.
He has brought it with him
from Australia, down under.
He has chiseled it from its place,
checked it through customs and flown

with it eleven thousand miles.
It is 2.8 billion years old.
When you heft it, you think
what you are holding should send you
through the seat of your chair, through
your mother's terrazo floor, through
Louisiana's hard, wet dirt, through
the earth's center and out into space.

But you go on sitting at the table.
There is the smell of boiled potatoes.
Your father is filling your glass
with water; your mother's head
is waiting for Grace. We mention
friends who will marry
during the holiday season.
We avoid the names of the recently dead.
We ask that no one give us details
of painful and critical operations.
No one wants to move
the 2.8 billion-year-old rock.
It is something to look at
when we won't look at one another.

## FAITH

What if the school children
on holiday in Audubon Park
are lost and are not afraid

while the pretty woman
who is to care for them
lets her skirt circle

her legs like water.
We want the seals
to turn their tails

into fans.
A man and a basket of fish
come to show us

that by adding light
to the seals' flat fans
we've crossed another barrier.

Now the seals are nothing
but light and the water
is no longer water and

my mother is no longer my mother;
she is the pretty woman
wronged and afraid

of the world. She is
the pretty woman
whom the chimpanzee hits,

who rushes her head
under the nearest clean running
water, who is forever ashamed

just because no matter
what she does, dirt
opposes her world.

# THE MOON AND NOT JAPAN

A pot of beans boils over because
the woman is waiting. She wonders

why it is she sees the moon
and not Japan.

A fish swimming behind weeds wears
scales to keep away the water.

Her own skin would simply absorb it all.
There must be a man who can walk through walls.

Above her stove a crucifix, spotted
with grease, lint stuck to it.

He needed that wound there.
This let his disciple see

his hand going in.
But if she could see.

Japan. A fan of fingers wiping
teeth away with a grin.

## KENO

Her mother's old and can't help herself.
Her father's sick, a bitch.
Her fifth ball keno
means big bucks, six,
seven, not bad odds
when even death, desire,
the usual obligations
can't stop her pacing
across the cards she claims
because they've won for her before.
Their numbers knit her nameless
children's names, the anniversary
of her godchild's first communion
or the last three digits
on her Buick's license plate.
Her husband died in a swimming pool,
too heavy and too wet to save.
She's been at it thirty years.
Between rolls she works
the paper's crossword puzzles,
she works whatever pattern
she sees appear. Whatever
she's done she's done
to hurry where numbers,
luck and the caller's voice
are more than she wants
to bear outside.
Her hands sink into circles
of colorful buttons; all around
her gamblers lift their arms
to roll the winning numbers
down. Knock, keno,
knock, knock, split pot.
Every night she knows herself
whether she's lost or won.
Every night it's not like life.

## YOU WHOSE BODY HAS NEVER TOUCHED
## ANOTHER BODY

The needle you take to sleep
shines on the saucer, what shines
in your sleep are the bedposts
your hands encircle nightly,
a lacquer your illness applies.
What shines in your sleep is the light
I bring to watch your body,
loose in green pajamas, lying white
across clean sheets, in the humidity
that sweats us.

*I have put together this world of 50,000 pieces.*
*I have looped nets trawlers pull*
*to bring life from underwater.*

You whose body no woman or man
has kissed, what sweat you've tasted
is your own, your hands are hung
around your neck, your twisted feet asleep.
You whose body has never touched another body
you teach me how to tend my body.
What few possessions you have held;
and those you're given you give again,
emptying your room for the room your ailments fill.

*I have painted by number to remind me*
*each detail is a number I count*
*and forget, count, it adds up.*

When you have poured white lotion to soothe
your cracked palms, you have thoughtlessly
paid me with geography, *rivers of milk.*
You have drunk rivers of milk to soothe pain
for pain's sake. Morphine means you wait.
So you have waited out the next catastrophe:

kidneys failed, liver turning you
into a yellow sign, your stomach satisfied
because it eats you piece by piece.

*In the dark I take up needlepoint.*
*My own stitches hide the holes*
*I fill with ducks, water, fish.*

You have done nothing since I've known you
but take these years to die.
If I cannot glove my hands with your skin
and bones, I want to rise out of this
body, bodiless I will love you more.

*I flesh in a fisherman in blue*
*who will always pull the season's prize,*
*whose eyes I've left unfinished,*
*whose eyes you've never noticed.*

# THE CONSEQUENCE OF WEATHER

The weather leaves wherever it was
and touches, this time taking

the shape of a woman's foot steady
on a cool iron bedpost.

What had been hot has been handed
the season's first cold snap.

Yet to permit the woman more of the same
her companion has tapped open her eyes,

risen and raised the window, turned back
the panels of curtains which frame

these points: a glass of water,
a hanging basket, a photograph of her mother.

The first is the nearly invisible,
the glass of water on the sill,

the visible well in which a toy giraffe's
perpetually dunking head reminds us

it is, after all, gravity that brings
us the seasons, that brings deer

down from green mountains to drink
from the stream which borders the woman's yard.

She sees the dish of light which is
the deer's tongue dipped in water

which changes by the second,
which will not be still.

The second, the basket, a tangle
of roots, moss, wire,

the hanging basket of wandering
jew, the pinnacle of the triangle

that is a relief after so many
unrehearsed lessons in the relative.

The plant's leaves, runners, shoots
keep undoing her botanical training;

when she would have them lush
and cluster at the basket's lip

they rush to meet the light and worse,
while she watches, the dead leaves move

in the morning's cool breeze
and the living are oblivious.

The third, what's left of her frame
of reference, the photograph

of her mother as she stands
on the steps to wave goodbye.

It is good that the woman
knows her mother's face well;

light casts a glare on the finish
the eye unaided can't erase.

She looks at her mother who was
always good with flowers,

who took care and gentled animals,
always patched what was bent or broken,

whose crooked finger never failed
to predict the weather,

who went easily into any water.

## COLORLESS, GREEN IDEAS

The color of broken stalks, they are
the wheat's sharp turn to hay.

They are the color of hospital walls;
patients sleeping, please, walk.

Will you wait, we'll try this once more.
They are some color. We keep getting closer.

They are our friends who sleep curiously
alone in their fine houses, gates latched,

surrounded by the dark which stands
like a horse in his stall, over them.

He stomps one hoof, any one of them
might wake shouting or unable to rise,

turn in waking's sad attempt to disengage
the dream's sentence, the night's quiet.

We think how difficult it is for nothing
to remain nothing. Everything resists it.

# WHERE THERE WAS STILLNESS

*Even stillness where there was stillness*
*consisted of hundreds and hundreds of moments*
*of motion that kept their equilibrium.*

Having seen cranes stand on cows' backs
surprise did not come in seeing the weasel

with a mouse in its mouth standing stock
still in the cabin doorway. Not that

this was any balancing act, the weasel
had four feet and solid footing

on dryboards on the threshold.
The weasel was white and this was spring;

its glass eyes and ragged fur told me
something cold had stilled it.

I saw a copperhead coiled around
the weasel's tail and wondered why this

was so contrived.
Because I am one to touch and touch again

I stepped forward to put my finger first
on the weasel's brow and so quietly did

the snake remove itself I saw the hands
which hold the brace and bit turn counter-

clockwise to be certain my heart
would be left a victim, not victimized.

## THE INNATE DECEPTION OF UNSPOILED BEAUTY

My silk legs give rise to bird calls
removing all evidence of my wish:

that those moments which the brain contrives
first to link, then to pull apart will find each

its place to settle, sink, sufficient while it turns
the scale toward no particular point.

Rather right on through may they desist
bedrock and proscribe their own boundaries;

some to forsake me, others to stake their claims
near those places in which birds knit

nests of grass fiber and fall prey to nothing
save their most natural enemies.

## SLEEPING IN CARS

Please think of a boy
tossing a ball
like you might toss
a coin into the moonlit
sky. Keep that in mind
or if you'd prefer
a bone bright with
a black and silver bow
before the full moon
while we move on past
the ramp's gore and begin
singing old one-eye-
on-that-open-road
we have driven across space
and once changed time
zones. The moon has struck
the leaves, even the dashboard
light reminds us
the ball has flown
from its socket and escaped
the oily limits of consciousness.
No one can see us
so we make good time
until the steel light
of the steep moon
shocks the girders,
braces, counterweights and cables,
the spans of light lifting
the Mississippi River bridge
and there it falls
that bouncing ball we tossed
a good ways back. It fills
the space sleep empties;
the homing device it employs
makes no bones of gravity.

## WORRY

Don Lupe is in the deep end
sweeping up the leaves

and scum so we can
fall into the water

without fear
for our lives

he'll have us pretend
gallons of water

appear out of nowhere
to cushion our blows

and difficult business
it's a pool full

of air and Don Lupe
sweeping a little tune

of worry away me
I am sweeping a little, too.

## GUESTS

Without a key we come in
to your house;

all across the country
there are houses,

full and empty.
They don't shift

with our comings
and goings,

they don't mean a thing.
We left our houses empty

to water the plants
ever after. All your plants

and your abandoned work
were in one room;

you were making our way
easy and clear.

Things go on without you,
it can't be helped.

The house isn't airtight.
Watch what we've fit

into this place or that,
how we lift what we move

and work against rest,
where we put the two

white monkeys,
salt and pepper, on your table.

# LATE AFTERNOON ON A GOOD LAKE

The water gives, it gets us
there, it gives to the footfall
while we catch our balance
to stand up in the boat
to begin to go where
the biggest fish fight
like nobody's business.
Skill and luck come
by different routes we go
by our own lights
and sun's light
leaves the water
to dazzle us so
that skill matters little
and luck is all around us
even when we miss
it moves to overtake us
it takes our gaudy lures
and tangles them in branches
high above our heads
or deep in water
bright because the lucky sun
stays with us a little longer
in the water the black oaks
drill their heights beyond
the other side and when
big fish mistake our lures
for food we bring them in
to the evening's light
which gives up to show off
the fishes' shapes and colors
because what we are
about to lose
puts its polished foot

before us and asks, *will you*
*no longer love me, look*
*what I shape for you to see.*
Two worlds without us
would not meet where we touch
look what we see when it is
evening and the ducks are
at rest we leave the fish
alone and turn to the ducks
who stand up for us and walk
on water while we chase them.
Look, somewhere luck is
shaking a cup of ice, I want
to drink that water.

# ALL WE HAVE IN COMMON

*Comment ça va, cher*
is what they all say

and we should
say thank you

it could have been
different it could

have been the same
we wouldn't have

changed the world
would have stayed

the same. I've sinned
and I'm bound

to do it again.
It seems only fair

to believe
what you know

is true. Let's forgive
blind faith and true belief both

wherever we find them.
After all, success is measured

sweetest down the road
you know where

we'll meet again.
Too bad

it's got to be like this.
Let's face it

it left us a little
touched. This world

is not the end of the world
and more than nothing but us.

## NO MORE

How the seven deadly sins
came to be no more is the story,
let's recall, of a study

of the day the rules gave
themselves a vacation.
The plot's as clear

as the back of your hand,
later we'll cinch it
for you, neat and clean.

It replaces *Your Right To Know*
by Sri Darwin Gross on your bookshelf.
At first it seems silly but picture

the sins in their vacation clothes,
how fussy they are with their dopp kitz
and tickets; they'd rather not go

but they're going first class.
They vacation to stuff themselves
and dream dreamless sleep.

Let's take a rest, be quiet
and listen to the odd assortment
of characters who take part

in this story. There's always
someone in love. There's always
someone with reasons they shouldn't.

There's someone who knows everything
and someone who knows better
than that. There's the coward

and the one who wants to be feared.
There're always those who believe
they're invisible and those who

throw water on everything.
There's always them and there's
always us. It's easy to say we

have more characters than turn-
of-the-century Russian novels.
But we don't want politics

creeping into this story.
We'll settle for *Citizen Kane*.
*The Ten Commandments*, Hollywood,

too obvious. Politics are
for the birds and the birds in this
story are the birds that test

the ease of flight in the shape
the wind takes as it takes
itself wherever space is

made for it to move the tops
of silver cottonwoods and green
hemlocks and Hitchcock's birds

in *The Birds* and buzzards.
Look at the way wind winds
around skyscrapers or circulates

curtains and light, the season
of opening doors, open windows,
vacation and rest. It's easy

to ignore the calendar pages flap
and the sheet of stationery
burning hard from the center out,

the revved-up hands of the clock,
and the comic effect of accelerated
growth, the hard fact of Precambrian

rock, each minute and month we mark
with a purpose or name, or claim
or see claimed by our band of sorry

travellers who agree birds like birds
in this story don't belong and
should be banned. But in this story

the sins are sent packing. Nothing's
banned. This is exactly how
it happens. *Sorry* and *common*

are key words in the story.
In one dictionary Louis Auchincloss
says *He brought the sorry news*

*of the terrible slide*
*in Georgia phosphates.*
For a split second we anticipate

a human disaster, common, decent
people or too many beautiful women
or, because no one understands them

and everyone knows they don't care,
the lovers slaughtered, pitched
beyond rescue under a suffocating

slide. For a split second
we're asked to go under with them,
test the earth for give,

strain to revolve our eyes
for the beam of the rescuer's lamp,
ask for help and hope if

we're asked we remember how
to drive away danger or deliver
the goods. But remember the sorry

news really concerns the economy.
In another entry we're given *sympathy*,
*grief*, *pity*, and *misfortune*. We see

*in a sorry attempt at apology*
how it feels to be *worthless*,
*inferior* or *poor* like the usual use

of the adjective *common*. We're
tempted to take heart when we see
it could give us the right to use

the waters and lands for fishing
and grazing. This story is so long
we need a green field and still waters,

we need a drunk herdsman to share
his oasis. There's more to know
about how the word *common* returns

to the lovers who, please remember,
were in danger. It shouldn't
make us like them more. They

don't earn our sympathy.
We'll never know if they'll love
forever, we'll never know if

they love at all. For the sake of
the story there's background
and biography, eccentric vocabulary,

the skim of the cream of the crop.
In the dictionary between *soothe*
and *sopor*, *SOS*, and *soubrette*,

*so so* and *sorghum* a herd of cows
bumps itself silly and *sorrow*
is among them. Their pasture

is lovely. Poplars are cool
in the distance and above them
the reseau blue of distant

mountains pulls us to follow
a clear stream where fish swim
into your hands as if your hands

held for the future
a set of unequal scales.
We've left out essentials.

*I forgot after we ate our tenderloins*
*we had ate our homely commons.*
We keep learning what they're always

saying, *our eyes are bigger*
*than our stomachs* is not half
bad. Please excuse us, we forgot

to mention four quarter notes
to the measure, we're not prepared
to take a simple knot for an answer.

Nobody wants a list of the deadliest
sins and a collection of their vacation
papers. This applies to both male

and female, to the delicious animals,
to the victims of accidents,
to our ancestors who spent some time

in the business, to the present
future and past, to life and
liberty, to property and to blood,

to taxes, and to fear of death
and will to fury and to disciples
and demagogues, to fear

of anything but death and
to *The Vanity Of Human Wishes*
and to the tonsure, to common stock

and shares of hide, to all we
sink our teeth into, to birds
and politicians, to the devil talking,

to *We're sorry* and *I'm sorry*
and to Romeo and Juliet, to the blind
poet who wrote "and what the people

but a herd confus'd/A miscellaneous
rabble," and to Congress and camps,
politboro and committees,

to the courteous and politic,
to *Two Citizens,* to the history
of as early as late last night,

and to forgetfulness and geography
and the astronomer's reseau and
to those who agree to inform

and to those who speak solely
in codes, who second guess and
won't look twice, who can't help

but lie and who want us
to say no, to yes-men
and to summaries, to symbols

which do not stand for anything,
to them and us, to you and me,
to your living hands as they

open in air or underwater
and move to be touched
by my equal desire.

## NOW WHAT

Am I supposed to believe
it takes the tangled

surfaces we mark to name
what is beautiful,

what is gainly,
what it is about

the red tiles whose lot
it is to let water rain

over their backs and bellies
and hide beautiful lizards

who do nothing
with any purpose

I can name
other than be beautiful

and fix my eyes
on their various steps

and glazed steps,
their darts and glances

toward their predators
who are themselves beautiful

and gainly creatures
like those of us

who walk with love
beyond these walls

the red tiles cap
and call who is this,

who is this coming,
who is this I believe.

# A GRAPHIC MAP OF ETERNITY

If it had been a snake
or the nose on your face

we'd be excused, exhausted
looking at the dead

who've got other fish to fry.
The dead are making up

questions too hard to answer
and they still don't love each other,

so leave the dead alone.
The dead have to eat

the pearly scales of the heavenly
gates, hold up the phosphorescent

bones, to be struck by the other-
wise simple pleasure, *we didn't plan*

*on our plane dropping us in*
*the frozen Potomac.*

The dead keep the peace
and they've got things to do,

so leave the dead alone,
they'll let us know

when they want us
they'll pull out their books

they've read with a vengeance
of customs and manners,

they live in the past.
Instead let us praise the past

perfect in its repose, immovable,
exclamatory and beyond belief,

past understanding, actions,
being or states of being

perfected before some definite
past time. This is what

I would have you promise me
you've cracked gravity's lock,

your desire to give me over
and over another chance to take

what's coming to us and the air-
plane in the air are distances

that are not so much like the flip
of a coin or the flip up the steep

rise of the odds against chance,
more like what we don't understand

made flesh, steel panels that engage
and emerge routinely calculated

to do what we can't believe,
that promise to get us there,

unbruised, beyond the Milky Way,
beyond the speed of light, cruising,

all the time in the world
without a doubt we'll be struck

when we see birds flock
like metal filings against

magnetic fields, and the mercury
of moonlight rising hot and cold,

the stages the sun picks out
before us when it strikes so many ways

at once, and the names
on neon signs when they shock

a name isn't it not beyond
belief when we love

the radio because it says
picture the music

it's hard to resist it
when you offer me a ticket

that crosses the distance
which divides us you give me

no choice in this
unpredictable channel

it's scenic water,
we're in this together.

Your hand is light and everlasting,
forbidden and skin and bones

and this is called praising
by the perfection of our bodies

this is called praise
when the dead and the living

invite the unborn to drive
or be driven without destination

past a lake where under a sky
broken by jet trails and beautiful

birds a speedboat drags a laughing man
whose figure cuts a pattern

of tracks in the water
that reflects the hereafter

what I would have you promise
what is too beautiful

not to mention this
is nothing special it is

the same elsewhere not
to mention everlasting.